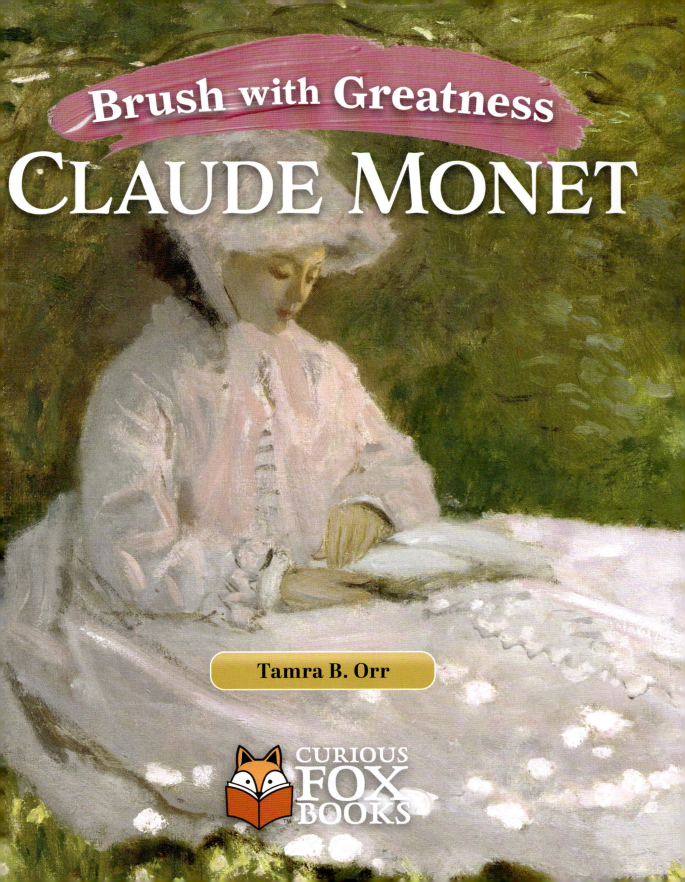

Brush with Greatness
Claude Monet

Tamra B. Orr

© 2025 by Curious Fox Books™, an imprint of Fox Chapel Publishing Company, Inc.

Brush with Greatness: Claude Monet is a revision of *Monet*, published in 2017 by Purple Toad Publishing, Inc. Reproduction of its contents is strictly prohibited without written permission from the rights holder.

Paperback ISBN 979-8-89094-160-2
Hardcover ISBN 979-8-89094-161-9

Library of Congress Control Number: 2024948652

To learn more about the other great books from Fox Chapel Publishing, or to find a retailer near you, call toll-free 800-457-9112, send mail to 903 Square Street, Mount Joy, PA 17552, or visit us at *www.FoxChapelPublishing.com*.

We are always looking for talented authors. To submit an idea, please send a brief inquiry to acquisitions@foxchapelpublishing.com.

PHOTO CREDITS: pp. 2–3 (background)—Shutterstock.com/Mr Twister; p. 4 (map)—Shutterstock.com/olenadesign; All other images—Public Domain. Every measure has been taken to find all copyright holders of material used in this book. In the event any mistakes or omissions have happened within, attempts to correct them will be made in future editions of the book.

Fox Chapel Publishing makes every effort to use environmentally friendly paper for printing.

Printed in China

Contents

Chapter 1
Monsieur Monet   5

Chapter 2
The Young Artist   9

Chapter 3
"A Veil Torn Away"   13

Chapter 4
The Mighty Trains   19

Chapter 5
Inspiring Others   23

Timeline   28
Selected Works   29
Further Reading   30
Glossary   31
Index   32

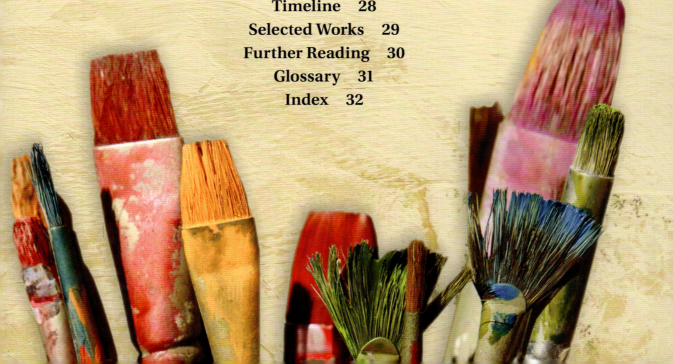

Monet captures the busyness and color of Paris without including every single detail.

CHAPTER 1

Monsieur Monet

"Gabriel!" my mother called. "Hurry up! You are going to be late."

Today was my second day working at the busiest train station in Paris. I swept the platforms where people got on and off the trains. The soot from the trains made the ground dirty.

Yesterday, when I cleaned the floor for passengers, I noticed a man who wasn't getting on or off the train. Instead, he was painting. I hoped he would be there again today.

Walking into the station, I saw the same man in the same spot. He had an easel with a large canvas on it for painting. There was a large box of paints in front of him. He moved quickly from one to the other, dabbing paint in all kinds of colors.

I had to sweep. But that didn't stop me from peeking over at his work every chance I got. I didn't see the purple in the smoke, but the artist did. The train station looked magical in the painting.

"Do you like it?" the man asked. He had a thick, bushy beard and wore a black hat called a beret **(buh-RAY)**. I nodded, a little scared to show I had been watching him.

He smiled. "I am Claude Monet **(CLAWD moh-NAY)**. Nice to meet you."

Monsieur **(miz-YUR)** Monet! He was a famous artist.

Monet's paintings of the trains coming and going captured the noise and power in the station.

Sometimes one artist would paint another. *Claude Monet Reading* was done by Renoir (**ren-WAHR**).

CHAPTER 2

The Young Artist

The artist packed up his equipment. He strapped the easel to his back and tucked his canvas under his arm, careful not to touch any wet paint. "The light has changed, so I'm done for the day. Do you want to talk about painting?"

I nodded eagerly.

"Carry my paint box for me," Monet instructed. "I like talking to other artists."

Me, an artist? I did not paint and definitely not like him!

As we walked, he asked, "Do you like school?"

I shook my head.

A Monet cartoon and his painting, *The Cliff Walk*, 1882.

"When I was a child, I would run away from school every chance I got," the artist admitted. "I would go to the nearby ocean," he added. "I love the sea. I would sit by the water and draw cartoons of my teachers." He smiled, remembering. "Finally, at age 11, I went to art school—and my life changed. Shall I tell you how?"

All I could do was nod.

Paintings like this by the artist Eugène Boudin inspired Monet to see the world in a different way.

CHAPTER 3

"A Veil Torn Away"

"It was not school that changed me," continued Monet. "It was meeting another artist. His name was Eugène Boudin **(ew-JEEN boo-DEHN)**. One day, I was watching him paint and something wonderful happened." He closed his eyes for a moment. "Suddenly a veil was torn away," he said, opening his eyes wide.

"I had understood—I had realized what painting could be. By the single example of this painter devoted to his art with such independence, my destiny as a painter opened out to me."

"You see, Boudin showed me the beauty that was around me—in the

Jean Monet on his Hobby Horse (Claude Monet's son) and *Woman with a Parasol* (Monet's wife), *Water Lilies and Japanese Bridge.*

fields of poppies, the ponds with floating water lilies, the rows of poplar trees. I painted my wife and sons at rest and play," said Monet.

"I began painting outside. I studied how the light changed everything and how everyday moments were perfect for painting." He paused to look at the river and the buildings we walked between.

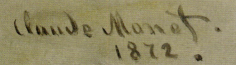

"Look at the light on the wall there," he said. He turned me around. "Look at the sunshine on the trees. Now, the sun is starting to set. Watch what happens."

As we stood together, watching the sun slowly sink in the sky, it was like looking through someone else's eyes.

"See how the yellow turns to gold?" whispered Monet. "Watch as shades of orange light up the leaves."

He was right. It was as if the light were a giant paintbrush, changing everything around me.

I would never see my city the same way again.

Monet's *The Summer Poppy Field* shows how strongly he paid attention to light and shadows when he painted.

Madame Monet and Child explodes with color and different shades of blue.

CHAPTER 4

The Mighty Trains

It was getting late and I knew my mother would be worried, but I had to ask Monet one question before going home.

"But sir, if you paint the world around you, why do you live here, surrounded by the soot and smoke of the trains?"

Monet paused. "As much as I loved my paintings, the critics did not. They said the colors were too bright—the scenes . . . not real enough." He sighed. "Those were dark days. I destroyed many paintings, even tossing them into the fire. But now," he added, the sadness fading from his face, "I have found a new idea—the trains."

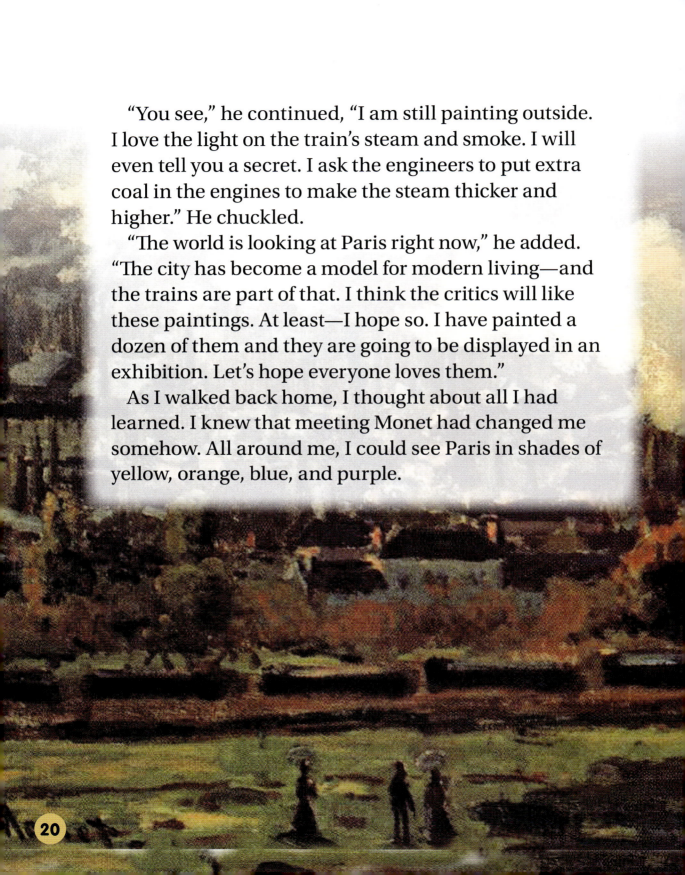

"You see," he continued, "I am still painting outside. I love the light on the train's steam and smoke. I will even tell you a secret. I ask the engineers to put extra coal in the engines to make the steam thicker and higher." He chuckled.

"The world is looking at Paris right now," he added. "The city has become a model for modern living—and the trains are part of that. I think the critics will like these paintings. At least—I hope so. I have painted a dozen of them and they are going to be displayed in an exhibition. Let's hope everyone loves them."

As I walked back home, I thought about all I had learned. I knew that meeting Monet had changed me somehow. All around me, I could see Paris in shades of yellow, orange, blue, and purple.

Some of Monet's train paintings showed the train from a distance, the smoke filling the air.

It was with the bright colors and shadows of Monet's *Impression, Sunrise* that earned some artists a new name.

CHAPTER 5

Inspiring Others

I continued to meet Monet and talk about art. He told me about an important show, where his painting *Impression, Sunrise* was displayed. A newspaper editor called his style "impressionist" and the name stuck. Monet, and the artists who copied him, were called Impressionists **(im-PRESH-uh-nists)**.

By now, the camera had been invented. Art didn't need to be an exact copy of life, it could be something brand new! Over the years, I saw just how much people loved Monsieur Monet's work. Many artists followed his lead to create works that were less

realistic—including me. After Monet's encouragement, I started painting, too!

Impressionists used short brush strokes of bright colors to show the effect of light on objects. Monet's series of haystack paintings were a perfect example of this style. Although each painting showed haystacks in fields, each one was unique because of the play of light and colors on them.

Depending on the time of day, the haystacks and Monet's paintings of them looked different.

Monet's water lily paintings were so large, they could fill an entire wall.

During the last part of his life, Monet's eyesight was failing. His paintings became even more like blobs of color. Despite that, he painted a series of paintings about the water lilies in his gardens in France. Each painting was different, as Monet showed the effect of sunlight and shadows. These huge mural-style paintings would become the best known of all his work.

By the time the artist died in 1926, his paintings were famous around the world.

Timeline

1840	Oscar-Claude Monet is born on November 14 in Paris, France.
1850–56	Monet attends school and meets Boudin.
1859	Monet moves to Paris to study art.
1861–1862	Monet serves in the military in Algeria.
1865	Monet meets Camille, who models for some of his paintings. Later, she becomes his wife.
1873	Monet buys a boat, which becomes his "floating studio."
1874	Monet's *Impression, Sunrise* inspires the style known as Impressionism.
1877	Monet paints trains in the Paris station Gare Saint-Lazare **(GAHR sahn-lah-ZAHR)**.
1889	Monet begins his water lily series, which he continues for decades.
1890–1891	Monet focuses on haystack paintings.
1911–1912	Monet's eyesight begins to fail.
1926	Monet dies on December 5 in Giverny **(jee-vihr-NEE)**, France.

Selected Works

1866	*Women in the Garden*
1872	*Impression, Sunrise*
1872	*Springtime*
1875	*Woman with a Parasol – Madame Monet and Her Son*
1875	*Red Boats at Argenteuil*
1882	*Beach in Pourville*
1891	*Stacks of Wheat*
1892–1894	Rouen Cathedral series
1899	*Japanese Bridge over a Pond of Water Lilies*
1900–1904	Houses of Parliament series
1908	*Le Grand Canal*

Monet's *Women in the Garden* is over 8 feet (2.5 meters) tall.

Further Reading

Books

Bjork, Christina. *Linnea in Monet's Garden*. New York: Sourcebooks Jabberwocky, 2012.

Danneberg, Julie. *Monet Paints a Day*. Watertown: Charlesbridge, 2012.

Krieg, Katherine. *Claude Monet*. Mankato: Child's World, 2014.

Maltbie, P. I. *Claude Monet: The Painter Who Stopped the Trains*. New York: Abrams Books for Young Readers, 2010.

Venezia, Mike. *Monet: Getting to Know the World's Greatest Artists*. New York: Children's Press, 2014.

Waldron, Ann. *Who Was Claude Monet?* New York: Grosset and Dunlap, 2009.

Works Consulted

Auricchio, Laura. "Claude Monet (1840–1926)." In *Heilbrunn Timeline of Art History*. New York: The Metropolitan Museum of Art, October 2004. http://www.metmuseum.org/toah/hd/cmon/hd_cmon.htm.

Brodskaia, Nathalia. *Claude Monet*. New York: Parkstone International, 2014.

Gariff, David. *The World's Most Influential Painters and the Artists They Inspired*. New York: Barron's Educational Series, 2008.

Murray, Elizabeth. *Monet's Passion: Ideas, Inspiration, and Insights from the Painter's Gardens*. Portland: Pomegranate, 2010.

Seitz, William C. *Claude Monet*. New York: Abrams Books, 2003.

Wildenstein, Daniel. *Monet or the Triumph of Impressionism*. Los Angeles: TASCHEN, 2014.

Internet Sites

Biography: Claude Monet
   http://www.biography.com/people/claude-monet-9411771

Claude Monet's House and Gardens: Virtual Tour
   https://3r-prev.com/mon23/visite-virtuelle/index.htm

Glossary

beret (buh-RAY)—A soft cap with a close-fitting headband and wide, round top.

canvas (KAN-vus)—Blank fabric on which many artists paint.

easel (EE-zul)—A stand or frame that holds an artist's canvas.

exhibition (ek-sih-BIH-shun)—A show in which artwork is displayed.

Impressionist (im-PREH-shuh-nist)—An artist who paints in spots of color to capture a feeling more than an exact scene.

monsieur (miz-YUR)—"Mister" in French.

mural (MYUR-ul)—Usually, a large painting made on or covering a wall.

palette (PAL-et)—A thin oval board used for holding and mixing paints.

parasol (PAYR-uh-sol)—An umbrella used for shade.

soot (SUT)—Fine black ash that comes from smoke.

Index

Beach at Villerville 12–13
Boudin, Eugène 12, 13

Cliff Walk, the 10–11

Haystacks, The 24, 25

Impressionism 23, 24
Impression, Sunrise 22–23

Jean Monet on his Hobby Horse 14

Madame Monet and Child 18–19
Monet, Claude
    death 26
    critics 19, 20
    school 11, 13
    train series 19, 20–21

Renoir 8

Summer Poppy Field, The 16–17

Train, The 20–21

Water Lilies and Japanese Bridge 15
water lily 26–27
Woman with a Parasol 15